WORLD OF PLANTS

FRANCESCA BAINES

How to use this book

Cross references
Above the heading on the page, you will find a list of other pages in the book which are connected to the topic. Look at these pages to find out more about the topic.

See for yourself
See for yourself bubbles give you the chance to test out some of the ideas in this book. They explain what you will need and what you have to do to see if an idea really works.

Quiz corner
In the quiz corner, you will find a list of questions. The answers to the quiz questions are somewhere on the two pages. Can you answer all the questions about each topic?

Glossary
Words that may be difficult to understand are marked in **bold**. These words are explained in the glossary near the back of the book. If you do not understand a bold word, look in the glossary to see what it means.

Index
The index is at the back of the book. It is a list of important words and subjects mentioned in the book, with page numbers next to the words. The list is in the same order as the alphabet. If you want to find out about a subject, look up the word in the index, then turn to the page number given.

J133, 125 /58
£6.32

Contents

All kinds of plants

A tall oak tree, a spiky cactus and a small daisy may look completely different from each other, but they are all plants. Almost every plant has a **stem**, **roots**, leaves and flowers. Each part helps the plant to grow or make new plants.

The key to life

We cannot live without plants. We eat them every day and make lots of useful things from them, including furniture and medicine. The paper in this book was once part of a tree! More importantly, plants make oxygen, a gas which is part of the air we breathe. Without oxygen, every living creature would die.

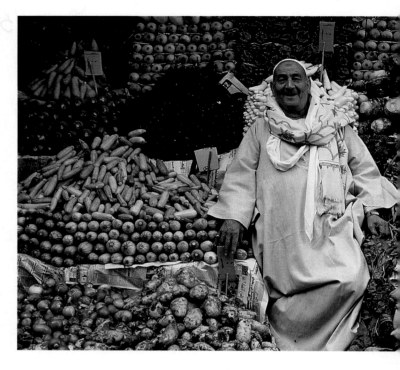

▲ Plants provide us with an amazing variety of fruits and vegetables. We eat **seeds**, roots, leaves, flowers and even bark.

Plants everywhere

Plants grow in almost every corner of the world. The most important things that make a plant grow are sunlight and water. In some places these are hard to find. In hot, dry deserts, it may rain just once a year, so desert plants survive by collecting and storing water. On the rainforest floor, there is a lot of water but little sunlight, so rainforest plants find special ways of reaching the light.

◀ Animals depend on plants, too. Giraffes use their long necks to feed on high leaves.

▲ Plants can live in cold, hot, wet or windy places. These plants are growing on a cold hillside.

Quiz Corner

● Can you name some of the plants that you see every day?

● Why do people and animals need plants to survive?

● What are the most important things that make a plant grow?

look at: Flowers, page 12, Woodland, page 16

Seeds

A **seed** is the part of a plant from which new plants grow. Seeds come in all shapes and sizes. A seed the size of your fingernail can grow into a huge tree. Conkers, pips, peas, nuts and grains of rice are all seeds. Some seeds are so tiny that you can hold over one million of them in the palm of your hand.

Sowing seeds

A plant needs to scatter its seeds so that they find room to grow. Plants do this in different ways. Dandelion seeds have hairs that work like parachutes so that the wind blows them away from the parent plant. Many seeds have hooks, or burrs, which stick to animals' coats and are carried away.

▲ When the seeds of the milkweed are ripe, the seedcase, or pod, explodes and the seeds shoot into the air like rockets.

▼ **This is how a sunflower seed grows and flowers. Why don't you plant your own seeds?**

In spring, plant your seed in a sunny place about 1 cm deep. Water it every day.

Soon, food in the seed makes **shoots** *and leaves appear above the ground.*

In summer, the plant begins to flower. Remember to keep watering it.

The middle of the flower is made up of hundreds of seeds.

Birds eat some of the seeds.

The stem twists so that the flower faces the sun.

A sunflower can grow up to 4 m tall. As the flower dies, cut off its head, scrape out the seeds and plant them the following spring.

SEE FOR YOURSELF

See how hooks, or burrs, stick to fur and clothes. On a dry day, put an old, thick sock over one of your shoes and walk through woodland. Take off the sock and see how many seeds with burrs are stuck to it.

Tasty protection

A fruit is a case that protects seeds. Many fruits have juicy flesh. They taste good, so that animals eat them and scatter the seeds in their droppings. When the seeds are not ready to grow, the fruit tastes sour and the animals do not eat it. When the seeds are ready, the fruit tastes sweet.

seeds

Quiz Corner

● Can you name four seeds?

● Can you name two ways seeds are scattered?

● Where on a sunflower do seeds grow?

● What is a fruit?

look at: Desert, page 22, Water plants, page 24, Food plants, page 26

Roots and stems

The **roots**, leaves and flowers of a plant are all joined together by a **stem**. Food and water travel up and down the stem to reach all parts of the plant. While the stem pushes upwards towards the light, roots at the bottom of the stem grow down into the ground, searching for **nutrients** and water.

Parts of a plant
Plants may look different from each other, but they all have the same basic parts.

Leaves and flowers ....
grow from **buds**
on the stem.

Plant stems usually ....
grow thicker as the
plant grows taller.

Roots hold the ....
plant firmly in
the ground.

Holding tight
Roots help to keep plants in place. In cold mountain areas, there are strong winds and there is often little soil. Plants do not blow away because their strong roots grip the rocky cracks, where they make their homes.

◀ Plants can grow in cracks in a wall. Strong roots push into tiny gaps to hold the plants in place.

Big and small stems

The size of a plant's stem depends on how many leaves and branches the plant has to support. A tree's stem is called a trunk. It must be strong enough to hold up long branches full of leaves and, sometimes, fruit. Small plants have thin stems that bend and spring back in the wind or when animals stand on them.

▶ A baobab tree grows in dry areas. When it rains, the tree stores water in its trunk, ready for the long, dry months ahead.

CHATTERBOX

Grapevines have found another way to hold up their leaves and flowers. As the stems grow, they twist and turn around frames or plants, using them for support.

Quiz Corner

- What do roots do?
- What grow from buds?
- Where does a baobab tree store water?
- How do grapevines hold up their leaves and flowers?

look at: Trees, page 14, Woodland, page 16

Leaves

Plants are special because they do not have to look for food. A plant draws up **nutrients** from the soil through its **roots** and uses these nutrients to make food in its leaves. The leaves take in sunlight, which gives them the power to make food.

Making food

A green **substance** in leaves, called chlorophyll, collects the sun's **energy**. This energy is used to make food by mixing together water from the soil and a gas from the air called carbon dioxide. This process is called photosynthesis.

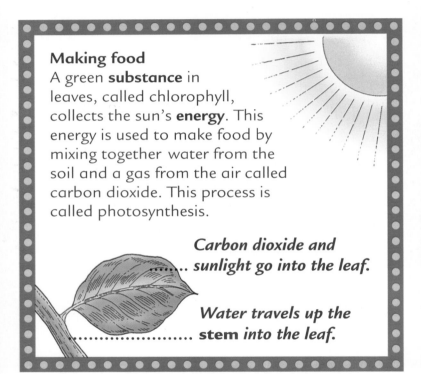

Carbon dioxide and sunlight go into the leaf.

Water travels up the stem into the leaf.

Wind and water

Leaves help plants to cope with harsh conditions. In dry areas, plants have thick leaves, or leaves with rolled-up edges, to help store water. In hot, wet areas, many plants have waxy leaves so that water runs off them and they do not rot. Often, plants in windy places have feathery leaves. The wind blows through the leaves without tearing them.

◀ Many animals get energy from leaves. Each day, a giant panda eats 40 kg of bamboo leaves and **shoots**.

Ferns and fronds

Ferns have small, fine leaves called fronds, which grow from curled-up **buds**. Ferns do not have flowers so they cannot make **seeds**. They make new plants by releasing tiny **spores**, which are usually on the underside of the fronds. Spores are so light that they are carried away to new ground by the slightest wind.

◀ Ferns prefer to live near the ground, where it is damp and shady.

Quiz Corner

● Which gas do plants use to make food?

● Why do some leaves have waxy coats?

● What does a giant panda eat?

● How do ferns make new plants?

look at: Seeds, page 6, Rainforest, page 18

Flowers

Flowers are the most colourful parts of a plant. They often smell sweet too. Flowers start to make **seeds** when tiny grains called **pollen** move from one flower to another. This is called **pollination**. Flowers need help from insects or the wind to do this.

Insect pollination
Insects enjoy feeding on **nectar**, which is a sweet-smelling juice made by flowers. When an insect lands on a flower to feed, its body is brushed with pollen. The insect flies to another flower, where the pollen sticks to part of the flower called the **stigma**. Then the flower can begin to make seeds.

▶ There are many different types of flowers of all shapes, sizes and colours. They all make seeds in similar ways.

People all over the world love the colours and smells of flowers. Flowers make good presents and some people wear them for celebrations.

Bees are important pollinators. Every day, they visit hundreds of flowers, such as poppies.

*The beginning of a flower or leaf is called a **bud**. This bud will grow into an evening primrose.*

*Pollen is made at the end of short stalks called **stamens**.*

Pollen from another plant lands on the stigma.

Wind power

Insect-pollinated flowers have brightly coloured petals and strong smells to attract insects. Grasses do not need special colours or scents. They rely on the wind for pollination. The pollen is so light that the wind blows it off the flower and carries it a long way. Some of the pollen lands on the stigmas of other grass flowers.

Wind-pollinated flowers, such as grasses, do not have petals. The wind easily blows the pollen away. ....

Quiz Corner

● What do insects carry from flower to flower?

● What is the name of the sweet juice made by flowers?

● Name a plant that uses the wind for pollination.

Meadow clary flowers have landing places for insects to feed from. ....

Insects land on the open flowers of daisies.

look at: Woodland, page 16, Useful plants, page 28

Trees

Trees are the biggest plants of all. They have strong **roots** which anchor them to the ground. Their thick, woody trunks mean that they can grow high above other plants in search of light. Trees live longer than anything else on Earth. The oldest trees are over 5,000 years old!

Food store

A liquid called **sap** flows through the trunk of a tree. Sap is full of food made by the leaves and **nutrients** collected by the roots. The sap is protected by a layer of bark around the trunk.

▲ Giant redwood trees are among the largest trees in the world. They can grow as tall as a 12-storey building.

▲ Most of the fruits we eat, such as oranges, grow on trees.

Falling leaves

There are two main types of trees – **deciduous** and **evergreen**. Each autumn, a deciduous tree loses all its leaves. In spring, the leaves grow again. An evergreen tree loses a small number of leaves every day. At the same time, new leaves grow so the tree always looks green.

CHATTERBOX

You can tell the age of a dead tree by looking at its stump and counting the number of rings. There is a ring for each year of growth. A thick ring means the tree grew a lot during that year.

▲ These conifers are tough, evergreen trees that can survive cold and icy winters.

Quiz Corner

● How old are the oldest trees?

● What is the liquid inside a tree trunk called?

● What is the difference between deciduous and evergreen trees?

● How can you tell the age of a dead tree?

look at: Trees, page 14

Woodland

Large areas of land that are full of trees and other plants are called woods or forests. In parts of the world such as northern Europe and North America, the weather changes during the year from a warm summer to a cold winter. Here, woodland plants have to cope with the changing seasons.

▼ This is how a **deciduous** tree grows during a year. You can see how the tree, and plants that grow near it, change with each season.

CHATTERBOX

In northern parts of the world, there are forests of **evergreen** conifers. At Christmas time, when deciduous trees have lost their leaves, people decorate conifers inside their homes. These are called Christmas trees.

In spring, young leaves on the tree are still small. Sunlight reaches ground plants so that they flower.

In summer, the leaves are fully grown. Few plants grow in the shade of the tree because there is not enough sunlight.

*In autumn, it is cold and there is not much sunlight. The tree stops growing and drops its leaves to save **energy**.*

Animals and seeds

Many animals live in woods and forests. There are lots of **seeds** and leaves for them to eat. Many unripe seeds are protected against hungry animals. Horse chestnut seeds, called conkers, stay inside spiky fruits until they are ready to grow into trees.

Lost food

Squirrels are useful animals because they store nuts and conkers in the ground to eat in winter. They forget where they are buried, so the seeds often grow into new trees!

*During winter, the tree grows **buds**. When spring arrives, new leaves and flowers grow from these buds.*

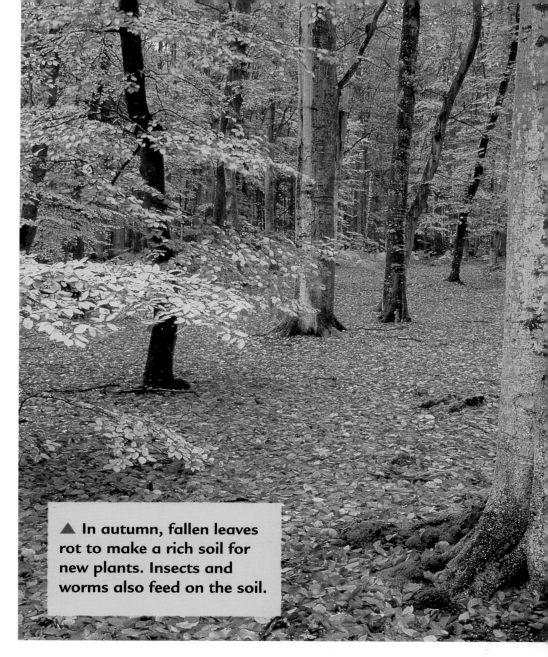

▲ In autumn, fallen leaves rot to make a rich soil for new plants. Insects and worms also feed on the soil.

Quiz Corner

- Why is it difficult for small plants to grow in a forest during summer?
- Why are squirrels useful forest animals?
- What happens to leaves that fall from trees in autumn?

look at: Leaves, page 10, Flowers, page 12

Rainforest

Rainforests are warm, wet places which are tightly packed with tall trees, leafy plants and colourful fruits and flowers. There are so many plants here that it is a struggle for all of them to find space and sunlight. Plants grow quickly because it is warm and there is plenty of rain.

Three layers

A rainforest is similar to a three-storey building. Each storey has its own plants and animals. The forest floor is dark and damp. **Mosses** and ferns are often the only plants that grow here. The middle layer is called the understorey. Here, plants have large leaves to collect as much light as possible. The top layer is called the canopy. Here, many animals live, feeding on leaves, flowers, fruits and **seeds**.

▼ Leaf-cutter ants cut leaves from the canopy and take them to their underground nests.

▲ Birds feed on the **nectar** of heliconia flowers, **pollinating** the flowers at the same time.

The ants use their powerful jaws to cut pieces of leaves from plants.

*Vines grow round plant **stems** to reach the canopy.*

Many orchids grow high up where pollinating creatures live.

▼ On this rainforest floor, green mosses cover most rocks and tree trunks.

CHATTERBOX

The titan arum is a huge flowering spike. It grows in the rainforests of Indonesia. It flowers for only a few days, so it has a strong smell to attract insect pollinators as quickly as possible.

Quiz Corner

- What are the three layers of the rainforest called?

- Why do some rainforest plants have large leaves?

- Where do leaf-cutter ants make their nests?

19

look at: Flowers, page 12

Grassland

A large, open area of land, where mainly grasses grow, is called grassland. Grasses are tough plants that can grow back after being eaten by animals. New leaves grow from the bottom of the plant, not the top, where they do on a tree. Animals eat the tops of leaves, while new leaves grow lower down the plant.

Wet and dry
Wet areas of grassland are called meadows. Here, many different plants grow because there is plenty of rain and few trees to block out the sunlight. Most meadow plants have bendy **stems** and strong **roots** so that they can survive windy weather.

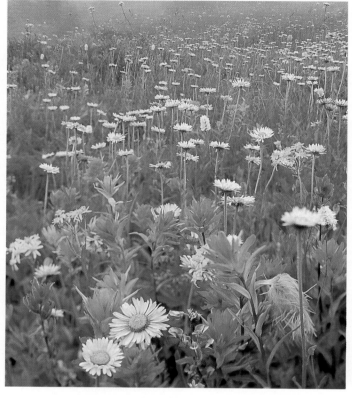

▲ In spring, this American meadow becomes a colourful carpet of flowers.

Savanna
The warmest and driest grassland is called savanna. There are large areas of savanna in Africa. Many different kinds of grass-eating animals, such as zebras and wildebeest, roam on the savanna looking for fresh grass **shoots** to eat.

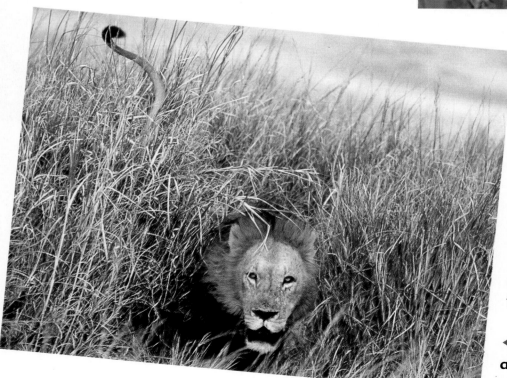

◀ In the African savanna, a lion hides in the tall grass, watching for **prey**.

20

Prairies and pampas

The prairies of North America and the pampas of South America are areas of cool grassland. The prairie soil is full of **nutrients** and people grow crops here. On the pampas, grass can grow up to three metres tall – taller than two children, one on top of the other.

Cattle men, called gauchos, look after herds of cattle.

Pampas grass flowers are tall and feathery.

▲ The pampas stretch across South America. Cattle feed on the grass here.

Quiz Corner

● Where in the world do you find savanna?

● Name three animals that live on grassland.

● What is the grassland in South America called?

J 133,125 / 581

Desert

All plants need water to live, but some can survive with only a tiny amount. In the desert, it may rain just once a year, so plants have found ways to gather as much water as possible and to store it for many months. When rain falls, many desert plants burst into flower and brighten up the dry and dusty landscape.

The clever cactus

Cacti are perfect desert plants. They have long **roots** that spread out just below the surface to collect as much rain as possible. They store water in their **stems**. Cacti protect their watery stems against thirsty animals by growing sharp spines.

▶ In the deserts of California, USA, many plants find a home on the dry and rocky land.

Prickly pears have pads of small protective spines.

Room to grow

When there is no rain, a cactus stem becomes thinner. These pictures show a cactus stem cut crossways.

After rain, the stem collects water and is full of juicy flesh.

As the cactus uses up the water, its stem shrinks.

The roots of the Joshua tree search deep underground for water.

Desert oases

In parts of the desert, there are wet areas, called oases, where many plants grow, especially palm trees. People and animals depend on oases for food and water. At an oasis, water rises from below the desert. The water has flowed underground from far away, where there has been plenty of rain.

◄ At this oasis in Algeria, North Africa, fruits grow on the palm trees. People take water from a deep well near the house.

The saguaro is the tallest cactus in the world. It can grow as high as a house. ....

CHATTERBOX

Small animals can dig holes in the soft flesh of a cactus. Owls and woodpeckers often make their nests here to keep their young in the shade.

Quiz Corner

● Where does a cactus store water?

● What is an oasis?

● Which animals sometimes make their homes in cacti stems?

look at: Roots and stems, page 8

Water plants

Plants grow in the water as well as on land. Many seaweeds and small water plants float freely in the water, while others fasten themselves to the seabed, or the mud at the bottom of a pond or lake. Along the water's edge, plants grow with their **roots** and **stems** underwater.

▲ A mangrove tree has special roots that support the tree in the soft mud along the river bank.

▲ Sea otters sleep in the water. They wrap up in seaweed attached to the seabed so that they do not float away.

Flowerless plants

Most plants that live under the sea belong to a group of plants called algae. These plants do not grow flowers. Some of them can be seen only with a microscope. Others, such as the giant kelp seaweed, can grow longer than seven lorries end-to-end.

CHATTERBOX

In boggy areas, the soil contains few **nutrients**. Some plants that live here catch insects for food. The Venus flytrap has leaves with tooth-like points along the edge. When an insect lands inside to eat the **nectar**, the leaves shut, trapping the insect inside.

Holding fast

The roots of a water lily are fixed in the mud at the bottom of a pond. The leaves grow until they reach the surface. Here, the leaves can gather sunlight to make their food. The Amazonian water lily has leaves that are large and strong enough for a child to stand on.

Quiz Corner

- Which animal wraps itself in seaweed before it goes to sleep?

- Can you name a plant from the algae plant group?

- Why do some plants eat insects?

- Where do water lilies fix their roots?

▲ Water lilies quickly cover the surface of a pond. The leaves stop sunlight from reaching other water plants.

look at: All kinds of plants, page 4, Trees, page 14

Food plants

Almost everything we eat is a plant, or depends on plants. Bread, fruit, sugar, coffee and chocolate are all foods that come from plants. Grass and other plants provide food for sheep and cows that give us meat, milk and cheese.

SEE FOR YOURSELF

Write down everything that you ate yesterday. How many plants did you eat? Try to find out where in the world they grew. Think carefully — foods such as bread and pasta are made from a grass plant called wheat.

◀ We eat all parts of plants. Carrots and parsnips are **roots**, oranges and pineapples are fruits and cashew nuts are **seeds**.

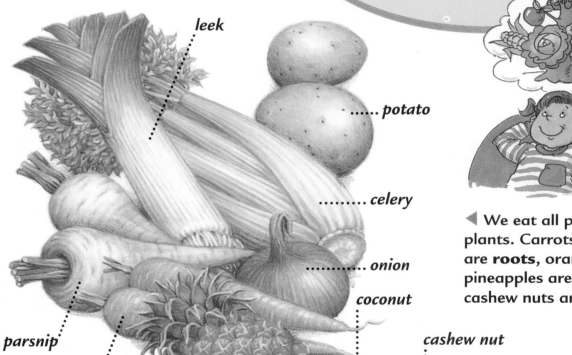

leek

...... potato

.... celery

.... onion

coconut

parsnip

cashew nut

carrot

banana

pineapple ....

orange ....

tangerine ....

sunflower seeds ....

.... apple

26

▶ In Asia, farmers grow rice in fields called paddies. The farmers flood the fields with water to help the rice grow.

Important grasses

The world's three most important food plants are all grasses – wheat, rice and maize. These plants are called cereals and their seeds are called grains. People grind grains of wheat and maize to make flour, which is used to make bread and cakes.

Helping to grow

Fruits and vegetables need warmth to grow. In places with cold winters, such as northern Europe, farmers grow plants in heated glasshouses. Inside a glasshouse, it feels like summer to the plants, so they produce fruit and vegetables all year round.

Quiz Corner

- Can you name four fruits?
- How do people grow rice?
- What are the world's three most important food plants?
- How can farmers make plants produce fruit in the winter?

look at: All kinds of plants, page 4, Trees, page 14

Useful plants

Plants provide us with so many useful things that it is impossible to imagine our lives without them. Every day we use things made from plants, such as paper, cotton, perfume, soap and furniture. Even the toothpaste you use may be flavoured with the mint plant!

Wearing plants
Look at the clothes you are wearing. Some may be made of cotton, which comes from plants. Are you wearing shoes with rubber soles? Rubber comes from trees. When the bark of a rubber tree is cut, runny rubber flows out. Straw is dry grass and is used to make hats.

▶ All of these things have been made from wood, rubber, cotton, straw, paper or other plant materials.

straw hat

T-shirt

chair

guitar

boots

shampoo

book

ladder

broom

basket

cardboard box

rope

rug

picture frame

pencils

baseball bat

medicine

tyre

newspaper

28

Tree farms

Wood comes from the trunks of trees. It is strong but can be shaped easily to make many things, from boats to musical instruments. Most wood is grown on tree farms, or plantations. Once trees are cut down for wood, people replace them with new tree plants.

▼ **This huge truck carries logs of wood from forests to factories.**

▲ **Paper is made from wood which is soaked and mashed up. This man is making spectacular kites from huge sheets of paper.**

Medicines

For hundreds of years, people have used plants to make medicines. Headache tablets were once made from the bark of the willow tree. Plants are still being discovered. Scientists hope that they will provide us with new medicines in the future.

Saving plants

Places where plants grow, from forest to grassland, are under threat from people building roads and houses or planting crops for food. Animals, as well as plants, are losing their homes. We need to protect these areas so that plants, and the animals that depend on them, do not die out.

Quiz Corner

- Can you name three things in your house that are made from plants?
- Where does rubber come from?
- What is paper made from?

Amazing facts

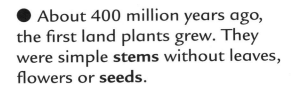

● About 400 million years ago, the first land plants grew. They were simple **stems** without leaves, flowers or **seeds**.

☆ *In 1954, a 10,000-year-old lupin seed was found in Canada, buried in frozen ground. Scientists planted the seed and it flowered. Today, scientists store seeds in freezers so that rare plants can be grown in the future.*

● The **sap** of the sugar maple tree is delicious! It is collected and boiled until it becomes a sweet, sticky syrup called maple syrup.

☆ *The flowers of the fig plant are hidden away inside the fruits. A special wasp lives most of its life inside a fig fruit and* **pollinates** *the flower.*

● The bee orchid has a very clever way of attracting male bees to pollinate it. The flower looks just like a female bee!

☆ *The talipot palm tree in Sri Lanka flowers only once in its life. After flowering, it produces more than 60 million fruits.*

● The world's largest seed is a huge nut called the coco-de-mer, which grows in the Seychelles. It looks like two coconuts joined together and can weigh more than three water melons!

☆ *Banksias are plants that grow in Australia where there are often bush fires. The tough fruits of these plants survive the fires and release their seeds only after the fires have died down.*

● In Venezuela, South America, people collect and drink the sap of a type of fig tree. The tree's sap looks and tastes just like cow's milk.

☆ *Over 900 different flowers manage to survive in the Arctic. Winter temperatures are freezing, but in summer the top layer of soil becomes soft and plants begin to grow.*

Glossary

bud A small swelling on a plant, which grows into a flower or a leaf.

deciduous A tree that loses all of its leaves each autumn.

energy The power to do things. Plants need energy to make their food.

evergreen A tree that keeps most of its leaves all year round.

moss A soft green plant which grows on damp soil, wood or stone.

nectar A sweet liquid made by flowers. Nectar attracts insects for **pollination**.

nutrients Substances that help plants and animals to grow.

pollen A powder made by plants. It is found at the end of the **stamens**, inside the flower.

pollination This happens when **pollen** of one plant lands on the **stigma** of another plant. The plant then begins to make **seeds**.

prey The creatures that an animal hunts and eats.

roots Parts of a plant that grow underground. Roots take up water and **nutrients** from the soil.

sap The watery liquid inside plant **stems** and tree trunks.

seed Part of a plant from which new plants can grow.

shoot A new part of a growing plant. Plant shoots appear above the ground.

spore Part of a non-flowering plant that helps it to produce new plants.

stamens Short stalks inside a flower. **Pollen** is found at the end of the stamens.

stem The long, central part of a plant that holds up the leaves and flowers.

stigma Part of a flower that receives **pollen** during **pollination**.

Index

Published by Two-Can Publishing,
43-45 Dorset Street, London W1U 7NA

© 2002 Two-Can Publishing

For information on Two-Can books and
multimedia, call (0)20 7224 2440, fax
(0)20 7224 7005, or visit our website
at http://www.two-canpublishing.com

Managing Editor: Robert Sved
Art Director: Carole Orbell
Senior Designer: Gareth Dobson
Picture research: Laura Cartwright
Consultant: Gail Bromley
Artwork: Gill Platt, Amelia Rosato, Teri
Gower, Mel Pickering, Peter Bull
Production: Adam Wilde
Additional research: Inga Phipps

'Two-Can' is a trademark of Two-Can
Publishing. Two-Can Publishing is a
division of Zenith Entertainment Ltd,
43-45 Dorset Street, London W1U 7NA

Hardback ISBN 1-84301-059-3
Paperback ISBN 1-84301-038-0

Dewey Decimal Classification 581

Hardback 1 2 3 4 5 6 7 8 9 10 04 03 02
Paperback 1 2 3 4 5 6 7 8 9 10 04 03 02

A catalogue record for this book is
available from the British Library.

Printed in Spain by Graficromo S.A.

Photographic credits: front cover:
Comstock; p4(t): Tony Stone, (b): Robert
Harding; p5: Planet Earth Pictures; p6:
Frank Lane Picture Agency; p7: Zefa; p8:
Bruce Coleman Ltd; p9: Planet Earth
Pictures; p10: Robert Harding; p11: Tony
Stone; p14(r): Planet Earth Pictures, (l):
Robert Harding; pp15/17: Tony Stone;
p18: Michael & Patricia Fogden/BBC
Natural History Unit; p19: Robert
Harding; p20(t): Tony Stone, (b): Robert
Harding; p23: Tony Stone; p24(r&l): Bruce
Coleman Ltd; p25: Robert Harding; p27:
Tony Stone; p29(r): Britstock-IFA, (l):
Tony Stone.

Title previously published under
the Launch Pad Library series.